LAUGH OUT LOUD

MORE KITTEN AROUND

Laugh it up, fuzzball!

By Jeffrey Burton

LITTLE SIMON
New York London Toronto Sydney New Delhi

LITTLE SIMON
An imprint of Simon & Schuster Children's Publishing Division
1230 Avenue of the Americas, New York, New York 10020
First Little Simon edition July 2017

Designed by Brittany Naundorff
Manufactured in China 0517 QUL
10 9 8 7 6 5 4 3 2
ISBN 978-1-4814-9959-0 (pbk)
ISBN 978-1-4814-9960-6 (eBook)

Welcome and get ready to **LAUGH OUT LOUD** with this **Animal Meme Joke Book** that's out to prove once and for all that wildlife are the funniest critters on earth.

Before you start, here are some helpful tips to make this book even funnier:

- give each animal its own special voice
- give each joke its own special delivery
- make sure you share the best jokes with your friends
- and don't be afraid to make up your own jokes, too!

C'mon,
World.

Oh no!
The human's back!

CAT MATH.

CHECK OUT MY LAMB CHOPS.

BUBBLE TROUBLE!

Real butterfly kisses are
horrifying!

DUH.

Too tired to cat today.

DUH.

BAD SELFIE.

DUH!

10 OUT OF 10 CATS AGREE:

They need to run to the next room for NO REASON.

(at all)

(like right now)

I swear they're Easter eggs.
Stinky, colorful Easter eggs.

let's get quackin'!

In the jungle,
the mighty jungle,
the lion steps on a Lego.

BAD SELFIE.

I know KARATE

and 100 other dangerous words.

Freed from the curse,
Marla never played
Duck, Duck, Goose again.

flamin-goes

wherever they want to.

HELP! I'M TRAPPED IN AN INVISIBLE BOX!

SWAFK.

Sealed with a frog kiss.

YOU'RE DOING
IT WRONG.

When dad tells a joke.

Okay, *now* I'm a little

COLD.

Now I just need
a tiny city to
DESTROY.

When someone's like,

PLEASE PASS THE CORN...

Only TOUCAN BEAK the

best you in the world!

MATH
GOT ME LIKE.

AIR GUITAR SOLO!
NEEEOWWW
NEER NEER NEER

WHEN YA GOTTA GO,
YA GOTTA GO.

Why doesn't the wild boar ever chase me?

STOP COPYING ME. STOP COPYING ME. STOP COPYING ME. STOP COPYING ME.
STOP COPYING ME. STOP COPYING ME. STOP COPYING ME. STOP COPYING ME.
STOP COPYING ME. STOP COPYING ME. STOP COPYING ME. STOP COPYING ME.

STOP COPYING ME. STOP COPYING ME. STOP COPYING ME. STOP COPYING ME.

LISTEN, IT'S NOT YOU,
IT'S ME.

I'M A CAT PERSON.

TRUST ME, KID.
YOU DON'T
WANNA GO TO
HORSE JAIL.

WHATSAMATTER?
CAT GOT YOUR TONGUE?

THIS GRASS IS MINE.

ALL MINE!

Video games count as homework, right?

I'm a turtle!

OH NO! VACUUM!

Uhm, I have a Question!

MONKEY FACT:
Liars don't wear pants on fire.
(They don't wear pants at all.)

Cat dentist says, "I can see you've been flossing."

WEIRDEST.
PIRATE.
EVER.

WHEN YOUR PARENTS
MAKE YOU SHARE A ROOM.

CHILL OUT,
I GOT THIS.

The majestic meow cow is

SPOTTED!

The trick is, you gotta

land on your feet!

DOG
WISH
YOU
HERE.

We run this roost.

Ya heard?!

Hi, my name's Randy.
I like long walks in the park,
back rubs, and chasing
squirrels up trees.

MUST.
SCRATCH.
EAR.
AHHHHHHHHH!

CAT

LEVITATION

THIS HAIR TASTES

SO GOOD!

HIGH PAW!

These aren't the right

PURRRRRR-SCRIPTION.

YOU GOT THIS!

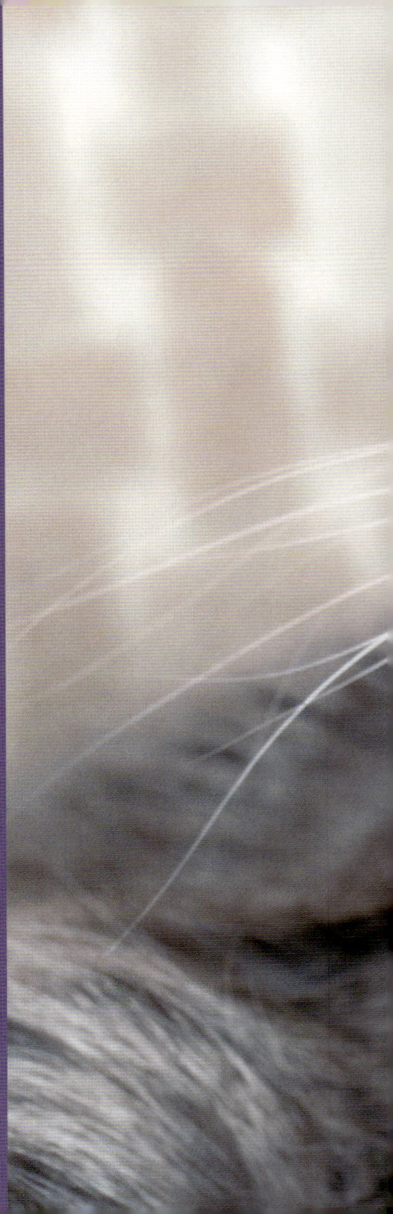

If you make a video of your dog, he'll think he's a movie star.

WHAT WAS IN THAT KIBBLE?

Nana nana nana nana
Nana nana nana nana
CATMAN!

I hope
cat doesn't see
this . . .

PRINCIPAL CAT SAYS GET BACK TO CLASS. RIGHT MEOW!

ONE DOES NOT SIMPLY
PICK UP THE CAT TOY
AND NOT PLAY WITH THE CAT.

BAD SELFIE.

I don't always pretend to be a cat,

but when I do,

I doo-doo in the litter box.

I swear I can't find the keys!

I know you farted.

LIZARD
WIZARD!

And you thought cowlicks were bad—

Now where did I put those glasses?

Good evening. I'm Klaus, and I will be your dog butler.

May I fetch you something?

That's right, Barbara. I know ALL your passwords.

I'm just sayin', don't stay out in the sun too long or you'll get

FRIED!

I'M HAIRY PUPPER.

BRAND-NEW COUCH, HERE I COME!

We're getting

a little

antsy.

Hello. I'll be your teacher this year and my class is gonna be . . .

RUFF.

KITTY LITTER
IN THE WILD.

Over here! Over here!

You with the honey.

Over here!

Aww, you brought me the treats?!

WORST. WORM.
WAKE-UP.
EVER.

I thought this was

a dance PURR-rty.

Ew, GROSS!

Don’t pet me with the same hand you used to pick your nose!

this is not a dog.

I'M INVISIBLE!

WAIT, DID I LEAVE
THE OVEN ON?

When mom
says smile
and dog says
SCORE!

Hey? Where'd the water go?

CAT MISSION IMPOSSIBLE

PUPPY VS. GHOST
BOO WILL WIN?

oh.

were you
Reading that?

GOTCHA,
HUMAN!

Oh yeah, well, anyone
can look cute lying down.
See?

allergies got me like . . .

Hmmm, do I detect a note of rocky road ice cream on the floor?

Me? Cheating?
Sir, I don't even know
how to play this game.
How could I cheat?

What are those neighbors up to now?

HEY, PRIVACY, PLEASE?
I NEED A LITTLE ME-OW TIME.

Wolf mom!
I found a
little girl . . .
can we keep her?

HALF CAT. HALF BABY.

ALL CRAZY.

BAD HARE DAY.

I BELIEVE I CAN FLY!

Eeeeeeek!
Something totally just touched my fin!

THE PERFECT KID TRAP!

You guys need anything?

Sofa!
CATNIP!
Yarn!

DID YOU HEAR THE ONE
ABOUT THE BRAND-NEW
TOY? I ATE IT.

Take my paw
and I will lead you
to the

SECRET CAT KINGDOM.

I KNEW I SHOULD HAVE

LEARNED TO SWIM!

I SAID,
WAKE UP!
IT'S TIME
FOR SCHOOL!

wanna hear something "bunny"?

Squirrel on a Surfboard?!

OH NO! QUICKSAND RUG!

LASER CAT STARE
ACTIVATE!!

I'M THINKING OF
HOW TO STEAL YOUR FOOD.

when your aunt
gives you clothes
instead of a gift card.

SOME DOGS SWIM . . .
AND THEN THERE'S KIBBLES.

No one sees me
in my cat fort.

DOGS ARE MAN'S BEST FRIEND?
YOU GOTTA BE KITTEN ME.

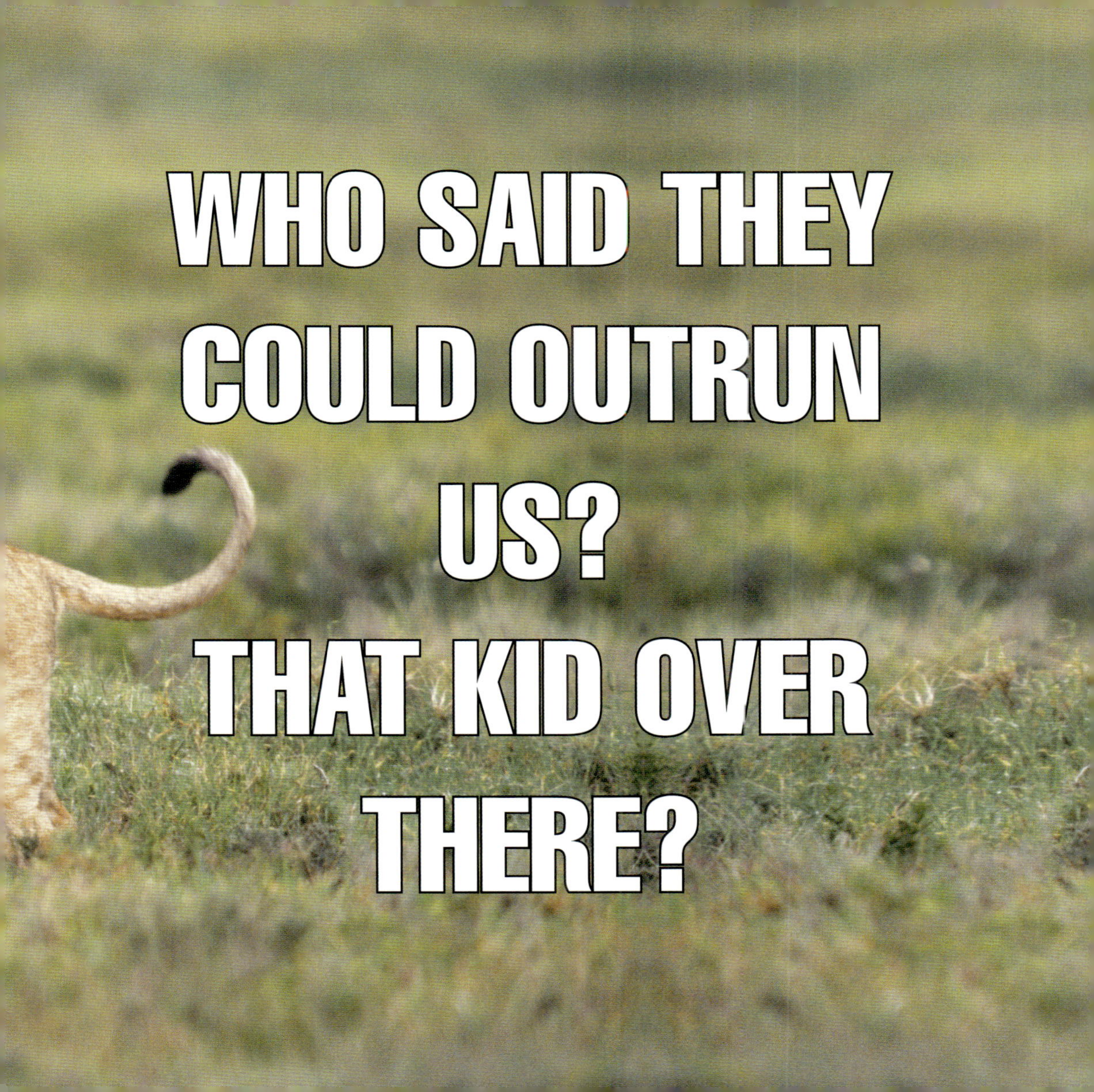

WHO SAID THEY COULD OUTRUN US?

THAT KID OVER THERE?

One time I drank out of the toilet bowl . . . and then licked your hands.

I'M NOT MAD, I'M
JUST HISS-APPOINTED

When your best friend picks someone else for the class project.

MERRY CATMAS

Okay, we pounce on the sleeping human in . . .
three ...

two …

MUST. BRING. STICK.

FOR. OWNER. TO. THROW.

Again we see there is nothing you can possess which I cannot take away.

I found
a
CAAAAAAAAAT!!

NO. JUST NO.

BAD SELFIE.

Toucan play that game.

STOP COPYING ME. STOP COPYING ME. STOP COPYING ME. STOP COPYING ME.
STOP COPYING ME. STOP COPYING ME. STOP COPYING ME. STOP COPYING ME.
STOP COPYING ME. STOP COPYING ME. STOP COPYING ME. STOP COPYING ME.

STOP COPYING ME. STOP COPYING ME. STOP COPYING ME. STOP COPYING ME.
STOP COPYING ME. STOP COPYING ME. STOP COPYING ME. STOP COPYING ME.
STOP COPYING ME. STOP COPYING ME. STOP COPYING ME. STOP COPYING ME.

#SPILTMILKDRAMA

Because some ducks

just don't care.

Oh great.
Becky's back.

Toto after the Wizard of Oz.

SNOW DOG HERE.

EVERY. MONDAY. MORNING.

WHEN DAD SAYS
PIZZA'S
FOR DINNER.

Purring contest in 3... 2... 1...

NO ONE MESSES WITH KITTY'S MILK.
NO ONE.

BAD SELFIE.

WHEN YOU FORGET YOUR
BACKPACK AT HOME.

WHEN YOU THINK OF THE PERFECT JOKE, BUT CAN'T SAY IT BECAUSE YOU'RE LAUGHING SO HARD.

I'm flying to the MOOOoooOOOoooOOOoooN!

JUST ANOTHER STEP BACK

AND THIS PICTURE WILL BE PERFECT -
WHOA!!

THIS BIKE IS A TOTAL
CHICK MAGNET.
CK MILTESI
CHAMPON
NUK
3

MegaPuppyYumzzz!

wait, how many fish are
in the ocean?

Good, you're here.
The litter box smells.
FIX IT.

On the road of life, you must always
remember to stop and smell the

BAAAAAAAAAAA.

NO.

Quietly plotting

EVIL PLANS.

A BEE?!
WHERE?!

That's right, James.
I stole your . . .
BRAIN!!

Nothing creepy about this picture.
Not. At. All.

I would like to buy your juiciest steak.

REVENGE OF THE
PIGEONS!

I know what you're saying.

TOADiLY.

I have no idea
what I'm doing.

SO HOT.

SO COLD. SO GOOD.

MINE!

Look at me. I'm a bee-you-tee-ful butterfly!

MONKEY FACT:

We're not monkeying around.

We're just going bananas.

WILD KITTYBROWS IS
HUNGRY.